She Sat But Not Still

SHE SAT BUT NOT STILL

by CAROL MOOG

All rights reserved. No part of this publication may be reproduced, distributed, or transmitted in any form by any means, including photocopying, recording, or other electronic methods without the prior written permission of the author, except in the case of brief quotations embodied in reviews and certain other noncommercial uses permitted by copyright law. For permission requests, write to the author at the email address below.

focusmoog@aol.com

Copyright © 2024 Carol Moog
Printed in the United States of America
First Edition

ISBN 979-8-218-50791-6

Cover Illustration by Carol Moog, used with permission
Cover and author photos courtesy of Ben Ross @benrossphoto on Instagram, used with permission

First Printing, 2024

For Julie, my daughter, my muse.

Mitosis

For Julie, on her birthday

Like a dolphin
Powering acrobatic undulations across the inside of the universe,
My universe that was yours
To use as cloud floats along the silken underside of the sky.
Dazzling in your energy and lightspeak
Of so much and so many weather worlds
Endlessly fascinating,
Never want to miss a moment,
How could ever be such wholeness that could be two.
Too, much too strong too sturdy too fragile
To long for the lengthening of time and yet live
As explosively within each time tick of every raindrop
Crystalline and transparent
Reflectant and opaque shimmer
Outflow gossamer threads of love to eternity
And bounce beam back to day earth.
Stretching gold swirling dust
Streaking the blue air with star pointing
The way out and the way in
To your future.
All beginning as you, incredibly,
Cell by cell
Soul by soul
One then two
Journey the rays of your own incandescence.
I pass the fire torch of passion and blood flowers and peace searching
To you while I keep my own
And blue flames turn green and then white

As we grow the bond and grow the strength as the heat heals,
Cauterizing against loss as the birthing
Begins anew and glows alive.
One then two
Mattressed to gentle the way when sharp edges are needed
One then two
Two dozen years
Of so much music
And so much dancing
And so much heartsteps
And so much truth
And so many gifts
Have we shared.
And will always
One then two
One and two

Contents

I.
Angry Red Planet	5
Remote	6
The Pocket	7
The Dig	8
Forged	9
Rage-Weary	10
Unruly Rodeo	11
Fellow Earthlings	12
Bone-Tired	13
Cheers	14
Wolf Warrior	15
War Chest	16
Mouse Power	17
Feral	18
Spring Fling	19
Significant Other	20

II.
Mirror Mirror	23
Orangutan Nature	24
Sorcery	25
Recess	26
Faithless	27
Line Dance	28
Carnival	29
Hallowed Victory	30
Mantis	31
Laughable	32
The Other Side	33

Hot Times	34
Conscripted	35
Off Road	36
Gladiolas	37

III.

Handled	41
Springboard	42
In Absentia	43
Offensive	44
Dipping In	45
Anemia	47
Be Advised	48
Bad News	49
Weathered	50
Reluctant Rapture	51
More and Then Some	52
News	53
Earnest the Clown	55
Musing	56
Noise Bomb	57
Being and Boredom	58
Trash Day	59
Game Over	60
Rules	61
Morphing	62
Surreality	63

IV.

Bombay	67
Being	68
Detritus	69
Reunion	70
Radical Inclusion	71

Secret Santa	72
Quitting Time	73
Free-Wheeling	74
Saved	75
Transmutation	76
Death-Defying	77
Playland	78
Childlike	79
Pinnacle	80
Identity	81
Self-Contained	82
Flight	83
Choice	84
The Blue Light	85
About the Author	87

Acknowledgments

This collection of poems emerged unbidden, in a flow of expression without regard for an audience. The notion of sharing it occurred almost as an afterthought. Previous poems were received positively, but these were different. It felt wrong to relegate them to a drawer.

I'm grateful to Wendy Ross, Abby Huntington, Irene McHenry, Jackie Cohen and Julie Holcomb for reading my collection. Always supportive of my writing, my sister Pat Vint was a big fan. Their reactions helped solidify my decision to publish the book.

My husband Roger's presence, humor and unflagging generosity fuels me everyday and grounded me throughout this process.

Special thanks to my highly attuned, direct, fearless editor Autumn McClintock not only for respecting my style but for banishing my hoarding of adverbs.

She Sat But Not Still

I.

Angry Red Planet

She sat but not still
Turning and twisting
Elongating her spine
Crumpling over her lap
Rotating her neck
Squeezing her shoulder blades together
Deepening sighs
Cumulus crimson
Images of Mars surfaced
The angry red planet
North star of her dreams
Remembering
Touching the scarlet cover
Tracing the black lettering
Checking it out of the library
Reverently carrying it home
Hidden in her bookbag
Racing upstairs
Consuming each page under the covers
Late
Very late
Midnight on Mars
Her true ancestral home

Remote

They wonder
How could she
So lively
Possibly be shy
In her basement
Layers of phantasmagoric images
Fresco the walls
Conflating
Amalgamating
Disparate fragments
Mosaics from her mind
Long ago she had nailed the door shut
Fearing being seen
She keeps to herself
Playing piano
She keeps to herself
There is nothing small
About small talk
Clumsy mumblings
Awkward lapses
Others chatter lightly
She produces a smiling face
Praying for invisibility
Still curious
They encircle her
She keeps to herself

The Pocket

Gnashing and gnawing
What did her rage really want?
Feeding it fresh cuts of violence
Sated it briefly
Giving her moments of peace
When she tried to leave
It sunk its claws into her leg
Refusing to let go
She soothed it with her own growls
It eased its grip
Hoping for haven
She pet its bloodied fur
And put it in her marsupial pocket for safekeeping.

The Dig

As rich as she was
Musically multilingual
Cozy with non-hominids
Her interior remained opaque
She needed a new tool
Despite having been on the same dig her entire life
Glistening painted shards
A huge collection amassed
Golden shreds of tapestries
Tiny intact bones
A born archaeologist
She shoveled
Continuing to search
Through barren stretches
Falling into startling crevasses
Treasuring fool's gold
Unable to diffuse ancient toxins
She needed a catalytic converter
More than a pickaxe
To breathe on her own

Forged

The brilliant blood orange globe
Drew her in with its lushness
Streaks of crimson clouds
Floated her closer to the core
To her magma
Trembling with danger
She felt the molten heat
Dissolve her boundaries
Freed from her casing
She began shapeshifting
Morphing into a new form
Her sacred Halloween pumpkin
Darkly malevolent
Its features blackened with her blowtorch
Giving it a sizzlingly Satanic flair
Forged from her own interior
Embodying her creation
She grinned

Rage-Weary

She couldn't just abandon her rage as it spun out of control
Flailing
Teeth-gnashing
Violent with terror
Never soothed by a loving caress
Or held until it calmed
Or until it cried
Driven to bite and tear
Starving
Desperate
Unable to wait to be fed
Knowing it had to fend
For itself
By itself
She took it on her lap
Put her hand on its arched back
Felt it relax its jaws and yawn

Unruly Rodeo

Determined not to allow her skiff to capsize
She positioned herself dead center
Paddling furiously
Riding the waves
Cresting with each surge
Detaching from panic
Reframing the experience
She willed her body to respond with excitement
Thrilling to the power of the water
Infused with her own sinewy strength
Controlling the course of her vessel
Pounded as it was by the roiling surf
The muscle memory of horseback riding
Gripped legs against the seat
She kept her head level to the horizon
Sky beginning to blaze sunset
Amber and rose gold
Igniting granite shoreline
Silhouetted dolphins
Pirouetting in time to her percussive pace

Fellow Earthlings

A carnival featuring live hippos
Graceless by Homo sapiens' standards
Balletic among beasts
Unstoppably skilled killers
Adorned with adorable ears
Capable of strafing huge stretches of water
Simply by exercising common toileting practices
Famously consuming watermelons whole
All sideshows slink away
Eclipsed by the voluminous anomaly
Known as the water horse
Ridiculed for its bulbous appearance
Giant razor tusks
Studding a gargantuan mouth
Ludicrous tail
Spindly legs
Obscene girth
Tufted rubbery skin
Belie its potency to destroy the naïve wanderer
Or the ignorant poacher
Capsizing boats
Drowning the unlucky
Or biting off their heads
Like watermelons
When gifted with a sighting
Appreciate who gets the last laugh
At nature's cosmic joke

Bone-Tired

She touched her knuckles
Feeling her boniness
Frightened to sense her own skeleton
A flash of anger shot up
How dare she die
Attempting to fire her engines
They sputtered
Leaving her sorrowful
And oddly compassionate
She used her body to grab life
Life used her body to grab death
Questioning who
Sick of being afraid
The hoot of an owl
Answered her

Cheers

Happy faces greeted her as she set up her equipment to play
People remembered her
Called out her name
Pretended to play harmonica
The drummer beamed at her
The band leader
Guitarist extraordinaire
Thrilled she was there
Simultaneously surprised and pleased
Awkward and self-conscious
The more she played the better
Inside the music
With the guitar and the sax
Speaking their language
Deep in the beat
On top of the melody
Intimate layering
Rapid fire comping
Taking it higher
Then she noticed
The crowd waving
Chanting her name
She flooded with excitement and dread
They cheered
Even after she left the bandstand
Bewildered and wobbly
She felt like curtseying
Strangely uncomfortable with praise
It would be helpful to have a hat to tip
A customary gesture
Eager to crawl back into the cocoon of her music
Where she could play her heart out

Wolf Warrior

Venturing out of her ice cave
Blasts of arctic air hurtled her backwards
Wrapped in thick furs hooded against the cold
She forced herself outside
Seeking her species
Breathing its musky scent
A timber wolf fully fanged
Stared into her eyes
Assessing danger
Stomach taut with fear
She felt no hunger
Unlike the wolf
Jaws agape
Love needing no reciprocity
Ferocious anima
The wolf was bound to her bidding
Howling
Snapping a rabbit's neck
Reddening the snow
Having met her guardian
She crawled back inside
Warmed

War Chest

She heard a twig snap
She was an easy target for the sniper
Her rage had been hibernating
Lolling around in contented quiescence
Until this moment
Galvanizing its weaponry
Rocketing toward the mouth of the cave
Infused with raw fury
Gut clenched against pain
Safely frozen
She smiled in satisfaction
Detached
Panting
She counted herself lucky to pack such protection

Mouse Power

Incongruously
She purred
Sitting back on her haunches
Before a delicate
Delicious
Baby mouse
Frozen snowball of primeval panic
Observing at a respectful distance
She waited for her instincts to launch her towards lunch
Nothing
She watched
Confused
She extended her claws
Sharp as ever
Hissed
Threatening as all get out
Salivated
Bristled her fur
Making her increasingly formidable
The mouse quivered
Flicked its tiny pink tail
Then darted into an invisible opening in the wall
Without a single piece nibbled out of its body
What had happened to her insatiable hunger?
What if she'd forgotten how to kill?

Feral

Soothing her feral self
She gently smoothed its fur
Petting it
Prehensile
It instinctively hung on her shoulders
Tangling with her hair
Roused and rapacious
Not wishing to slow its feeding
She offered tasty treats
Blood orange
Marrow
Grubs
Sweetbreads
She adored her primal nature
Always there to defend her
Nested and waiting
Its claws digging deliciously into her scalp
Raking through her trailing tresses
Urged alive

Spring Fling

At the extreme top of the roller coaster
Her breathing quickened anticipating the abandon
Flinging her out of the tiny metal container
She white-knuckled the bar
Plummeting
Ears ringing with the shrieks of others
Arms held daringly above their heads
Dizzied with the pounding of her heart
Stomach churning free fall weightlessness
Relishing in the terror was unfathomable
No hope of rescue
Irrevocable
Careening around hairpin turns
Knees banged the sides of the death chamber
Squeals of glee pierced the atmosphere
Willing herself not to vomit
She clenched her gut
Steel muscles
Lurching to the finish
Utterly disoriented
Legs numb
Stumbling out
She dragged herself to a wooden bench
Clinging to it like a life raft
Lodging a long splinter deep in her hand
Antiseptic wipes
Tweezers
Band-aids
Relieved by reality

Significant Other

For the first time in several agonizingly long years
She dared to work out at the gym
Maskless
Breathing easily as she jogged faster
Accelerated intensity
She felt startlingly normal
Going there every day
Well known and familiar
Always with a face covering
Nonplussed to enter this new old world seamlessly
Expecting comments and surprised observations
There were none
Greeted as if still masked
Or never masked
It was as if nothing had happened
No hiatus
Life had been going on exactly the same
Everyone had long returned
To the extraordinary ordinary
Finally as she was leaving
One she knew smiled and spoke
You have a very nice face

II.

Mirror Mirror

Her changing body apparently
Was staying put
Unless faced with a mirror
She was detached from this motley image
She felt strong and lithe
Blithely running her life at the same perky pace as ever
Yet
The mirror reflected wrinkly data
It assaulted her sense of self
As youthful
Glancing briefly enough to glimpse the truth
Long enough to admit its presence
Short enough to flee its impact
Honestly enough to know the irony
Retroactively she mused if exiling her age would damage her
Rupture reality
If only she could age without looking older
If only she could not age and live forever
If only she could find beauty in her aging self
She could break all the mirrors
But then how could she put on make up to look younger?
The dilemma was deleterious
What a cosmic joke
Laughing at herself
Perfect punchline

Orangutan Nature

Restless
Long orange fur flowed
Looking incongruously like yak wings
Swinging between branches piercing the jungle canopy
Soft gaze into the rainforest
Swarming
Thick with jade figs
Dotted with tasty ant tidbits
Leading to hands of bananas
Ripe for the taking
Hammocking her lumbering body
Lolling against the ficus tree
Sated with succulents
Clambering down
She trapezed her way to the tangled earth
Scampering and rolling
Unencumbered acrobatics
Resonant howls
She raced alone
Grasping vines and pulleying upwards
High into her woven world

Sorcery

The fleeting
World-class insignificant
Details of each day
The briefest glance
The lightest grazing of eye contact
Enthralled her
In full meltdown misery
A child tries to disappear into a blue carpet square
Shaping his body like an armadillo
Exposing no soft underbelly to the bristling environment
In his haste to escape
One foot was naked
Approaching cautiously
Closing the gap inch by inch
Holding his shoe
She placed it in his outstretched hand
It was a mutual victory
A moment of sorcery
He smiled
That morning a magician had amazed the class
How did you do that?

Recess

Playing leapfrog with her synapses
Coherent thoughts hide in her amygdala
Where they do pratfalls and make each other laugh
Pinkish grey and shiny
Her cerebrum loosens its grip
Quitting keeping the kids quiet
Play explodes
Rolling ropes of clay
Draping it on their faces
Putting it in their mouths
Making airplanes out of lettuce
Stomping on raisins
Sprinkling sugar on hotdogs
Draping toilet paper on foliage
Inviting newts to the table
Demanding to know why
Never wanting answers
Only to play with questions
Since everyone knows no one knows

Faithless

Being envious of those who had faith
She envisioned seeking god
A white egret opened its wings and beckoned
To mount and soar
Weightless one with the sky
Ever-receding blue marble
She was on her way
Way to what?
She wasn't at all ready to find god by dying
Which is what the scene was shaping up to be
High speed travel
Light tunnel
She just wanted a sign of comfort
Her kind of god
The god of don't worry
I got you
Enlightenment wasn't billed as the path to reassurance
Enlightenment offered radical acceptance of doom
She kicked the egret's sides and steered it back to earth
The barest of ripples
Quietest of splashdowns
Sliding off she swam to shore
Unencumbered by divine intervention

Line Dance

Perhaps this is out of line
Not flinging herself on the floor screaming
Perhaps this is out of line
Eating time
Each minute
Sixty of them
One whole hour
One whole song
Dumdadumdum
Perhaps this is out of line
But each measure
Torn into tiny pieces
Slo-mo
Studied
Serially
Kills brain cells
Perhaps this is out of line
Waving weakly from the couch
The prone drummer twitches
She opines
Maybe
We could try another song
Leaping to his kit
He sets a funk beat in motion
At last

Carnival

The insouciance of women wearing scarves
Completely elusive
Adorning herself with a scarf
She constantly arranged, tucked, pulled, gathered
Her entire being was at its mercy
She was odd
Others bounded from their vehicles in one smooth motion
Put together
She bumbled out
Bags dangling from both shoulders
Extra coats bunched under her arms
Kleenex bulging out of pockets
She was odd
At social events she loitered by the food
Eying the offerings suspiciously
Trying to identify edibles
A useful time-consuming task
Spying a straggly gangly teen
Head resting on the table
Warmed her heart
We're all freaks at the core
She had an affinity for unmasked misfits
Looked for eccentrics she could invite to her personal carnival
Insect collectors like herself
Tadpole videographers
Rock pilers
Bubblegum blowers
Python hunters
Drummers playing wrought iron railings
Mental and physical contortionists
All are welcome

Hallowed Victory

Knowing her aversion to venomous insects
He did not agree with her perspective
Clad in apiary spacesuit splendor
Armed with gleaming pickaxe
He plunged its metal teeth into the living hive
Releasing swarms of overwrought yellowjackets
Prowling the battlefield
Unhurried he dismantled their subterranean residence
Scattering wood from their rotting tree stump
He moved on to each neighboring nest
Ferociously followed by battalions of wasps
As if in a fugue state
Merged with his mission
He stabbed his weapon into the depths
Catalyzing the attack of hundreds more
Unperturbed
Covered with stinging creatures doing their best to kill him
He rid her yard as requested
Later that week
He brought her a bundle tied with a white ribbon
Candlesticks made of rolled sheets of beeswax
Humbling
Exquisite

Mantis

Crouching inside the feathery cave of weeping willow limbs
She witnesses
Exoskeleton camouflaged greens and brown
The praying mantis
Nearly imperceptible
Stand on its massive back legs
Clasping a black-backed beetle
Nibbling it like an ear of corn
This spectacle of a lifetime
Feasting on each minute detail
Privileged with this performance
She dare not move a hair
Finishing its meal
It turns its triangular head
Staring directly into her eyes
Folding her hands in prayer
She bows to this supreme predator

Laughable

Now more than ever
Being grateful was the only game in town
Complaining about anything at all
Given the cornucopia of her life
Was unseemly at best
Toxic at worst
Transforming deficiency into abundance
Beyond Herculean
Blinded to her riches
Ancient starvation made her suspect sustenance

Now more than ever
Offerings of love
Lingering longer in joy
Welcomed warmth
Opened pathways
She needed to take humor seriously
At its core
Criticism was unfunny
Born with the gift of laughter
(She was told)
Now more than ever
She was meant to use it
Now more than ever
She was meant to share it
Gratitude
Might be more fun

The Other Side

Walking on the same trail
Wearing the same high-top sneakers
Suddenly looking through a Vu-Finder
Cataract surgery
Dumbstruck by details
Tiny variegations in bark, pebbles, flowers, grass, crumpled
 paper, dirt
Dazzling
Flooded by neon colors
A stop sign blared its red and white like a siren
An alarm urging her to run
But she hadn't run
Cataract surgery
Lifted the veil
Revealing the sparkling drops of dew on a dandelion
And like a river of obsidian
Words flowed from her pen
As she watched her hand write
Studying each blue vein
Stripped of her blurry buffer
She felt strangely naked
Light ricocheting off an empty beer can
Sent her reeling
Then she felt the familiar trail mix in her pocket
Grounded
She crunched her way back home

Hot Times

Melting into the couch
Limbs elongated like hot taffy
Sliding along the floor
Vertebrae provided no armature
Her body pooled into a molten mass
The intensity of morning heat
Fed the burgeoning caldron of the afternoon
Building to the firestorm of the evening
Losing no degrees to darkness
Promising more at dawn
Fueling the earth's vengeance
Magma flowed dangerously close to the surface
Burning the feet of those species daring to perambulate
Struggling to think clearly
Her mind sweltered
Swallowed up in blazing shambles
Sporadic relief in random rooms
Cooled by vintage air conditioners
Bookended by memories of tropical trips
Historically delightful vacations
Currently featuring life in Hades
Even abandoned by Satan
Wisely on holiday
Touring Antarctica
Grinning ghoulishly at the globe

Conscripted

Bombarded by battalions of minute beetles
She is unable to casually eat her salad
Tiny bugs land on every leaf
Drown in her dressing
Crawl into her wine glass
Spelunk into the alveoli of her bread
Her dinner companions shoo them away
This is not an ordinary nuisance of outdoor dining
This is a rampage
Wriggling bodies rain down
Social graces completely eclipsed by the drive to counterattack
She plucks dying insects from her water
Impales them on her fingernails
Slaps them on her arms
Mummifies them in her napkin
She is alone in her animation
An obvious example of her alien nature
Others simply adapt to the infestation
To her a cause de guerre
If her vigilance falters
More will be consumed with her Amatriciana
Already she feels unordered protein bits writhing in her gut
Her rational mind knows the simple truth
She sits beneath a tree nesting the invaders
Her inner crazy knows she is an experimental subject
Tested for composure under enemy fire
Celebrating her success in not flipping the table over
She awards herself a Conspicuous Gallantry Medal
And pats herself on the back
Smashing a lone sniper in the process

Off Road

No trail
Refusing to allow fear to halt her adventuring
She forged ahead
Bending the rules by ignoring them
Slashing swaths in the matted forest
Turning sideways to slip through
Running now caressed by lush leaves
Like cilia
Undulating her into the clearing
Boundlessly meadowed dense with flowers
Sequined oasis of sunshine
A luna moth
Velvet winged peridot
Opened

Gladiolas

Huge purple blooms
Flower finery at its best
The cliche of gladness
Flounced shamelessly
She'd been busy blurring the boundary
Between the moss-green rug and the algae ottoman
Verdant versions of the forest floor
Heaving molecules in motion
Riding the undulations
Lulled into fatigue
Ceasing serial pursuits
Ten minutes ago
Stillness came easy
The way forward
Strewn with long stalks of purple
Two choices only?
Walk through them
Stained by their color
Or move them aside, create a path
Untouched
Instead
She dropped to the ground
Rolling her body in the petals
Saturating her skin
Splotched and glowing
She slipped into the garden
Made herself quite glad
And invisible

III.

Handled

As long as she held her own hands
Folded in her lap
Her rage receded
Her arms warm
Body relaxed
If she had been held while raging as a child
Her cells could have absorbed the anger
Like sponges in surgery absorb the blood
To not flood
The patient
But she was always drowning
Her helplessness a tsunami
Overwhelming her and then spitting her out
Gasping for breath on an empty beach.
But when she held her own hands
She was whole

Springboard

Standing at the end of the board
At the very top of the high dive
Was never a goal
Never fathomable let alone desired
Finding herself
Springing up
Cutting through the air like a rapier
Headed straight for tourmaline waters
Slicing the silken surface
Shockingly
She popped up
Laughing
She abandoned the fear ballasting her life
She defied gravity and jumped through the sky

In Absentia

Holding my face in my hands
A mother's kiss
Absent
My skin softly alive

Outlier in Bowlby's research
Babies failing to thrive with unheeded cries
I lived
Underneath the rage
Loneliness
I don't want to leave her alone
The lonely one
The lonely me
She belongs to me
She longs to be me
She longs to be with me
I need to hold her
Quickly I guard her from the unlovable monster
Teeth bared
I protect her
Even from myself

Offensive

Quills on full alert
At the first touch of danger
The porcupine released its sheath
Into the flesh of the offender
Daring to come too close
Accustomed to these strikes
Culminating with this latest onslaught
The cautious intruder
Claimed no injurious intent
Backing away
Holding up a mirror as a shield
Alien remorse stabbed the porcupine
Facing a reflection of its relentless rage
Flattening its quills
It waited
A tattered olive leaf extended
The prickly rodent nibbled
Humbled by kindness
An amicable armadillo

Dipping In

Surrounded by smiling mostly strangers
She meanders studying
A creamy dip with brownish flecks
Shiny pink flesh on round crackers
Little triangular sandwiches with green filling
Deciding what looks familiar enough to taste
Like a piece of yellow cheese
Discerning what ingredients she recognizes
Like olives
Identifying what she loathes
Like fish
Milling past people barely glancing up
Moving room to room
Outside to inside
Reading meaningless name tags
Stopping at the first child she notices
Triple dipping chips into salsa
Licking his fingers before using them as guacamole scoops
Jabbing a sugar snap pea into hummus
Chewing the end and swirling it around for some more
Avoiding pureed germ dip
She chortles with the child
Anchored at last
She tries joining a conversation about kayaking
Just that morning buffeted by sudden high winds
She wants to share her panic
They want to share Pine Barren politics
A young mother horsing around with her kid catches her eye
She jumps into the fray
Laughing

Celebrating the birth of an ebullient friend
A bagpipe player regales the crowd
Weaving weird sonorous moans
Men in kilts dance
Songs burst forth
Candles on many cakes exuberantly extinguished
Merging with the music and the joy

Anemia

Usually springy
Something deadened her bounce
Pulled her down
Fatiguing her spirits
Musically impoverished
She grieved for blues
For the deep groove
Of wordless intimacy
The silent desert
Starved her
Hungry for the beat
Listening was no proxy for creating
Unaware of how gaunt she had grown
Filling herself with facsimiles
Until the loss gnawed a jagged hole
Releasing a flow of heat
Freeing her to swim towards the sound
Drums beat her name

Be Advised

Act your age
What a strange concept
Who decides how an age acts?
She joins dancers in Venezuela
Plays harmonica with drummers in Namibia
Catalyzed by the moment
Is eating live ants in Australia age-inappropriate?
Kids assign her many different numbers
Some are big and many are not
One is shocked
You play with children??
Wrinkles count
Except when they become laugh lines
The best comedians are kindergarteners
Toilet humor always funny
Her age sat under a clock
While she ran off to recess

Bad News

There was simply no way to live fully enough to not die
Taking advantage of every audacious opportunity
Sucking the marrow out of every minute
Dancing her heart out until she collapsed
If Princess Di could die
So could she
So would she
A Buddhist meditation invites
Intimately imagining each stage of decay
Rotting flesh
Maggots
Bleached bones
Disinclined to accept this mortality tour
She tried treasuring everyday lowly moments instead
A pile of paper clips that she would never see again
Dishes loaded haphazardly
Mocking her superior design
A stone water-etched with a perfect cross
Barring a chipmunk tunnel
Nothing was too insignificant to be missed
None of this inched her closer to enlightenment
It was the same as it had always been
Trashed or treasured
Death took it all
Which pissed her off
She didn't like the arrangement

Weathered

Slicing the black sky
A jagged-edged whip of lightning connected with the earth
Struck with awe
She stayed put
Uniquely unafraid
Pausing her predictable panic
Seated under a dripping awning
Rain sluiced the air
An impromptu sound and light show
Conjured the Parthenon at night
Relishing her spanakopita
She dipped bread in olive oil
Not long ago she would run from this danger
Now ignited by the electrical storm
Her heart pounded with thunder

Reluctant Rapture

On safari
Close enough to feel the rush
Lions chasing a lone wildebeest
Out of nowhere
A pounding herd ransacked the clearing
Splitting the world like the Red Sea

Wave after wave of deafening heartbeats
Shot through her body
Convulsing her
Palpable infinite exigency
Love everyone
Even that one

Repulsed
She did not want to
Swept into surrender
Wordless

More and Then Some

A golden temple in Burma
Walking barefoot up sacred guano encrusted steps
Green light drenched rainforests in Belize
A leaden boa dangling from her neck
A Namibian village throbbing with drummers
Lotus flowers aflame floating on the Ganges
Towering suspension bridges
Swaying transport to an Amazon treehouse
Felucca at sunset in Lamu
Walking the hemlock path of death with Socrates
Being swallowed by Santorini's fiery sunset
Riverboating through the mosaic of the Mekong
Clambering into the heart of Egypt's pyramids
Falling asleep in pitch black fear
Hunkered down in a dugout canoe
Barreling towards Angel Falls
Prehistoric dancers at the sing-sing in New Guinea
She was the thread snaking through it all
Relishing her National Geographic life
Puzzling where to go next
Harmonica in Havana
Again

News

Living inside her customary bubble
Laser focused
Balancing on one foot required total concentration
Getting it exactly right
Allowed no peripheral vision
Satisfied
She allowed herself to pivot
Eying the pull-up bar
On the way she noted an aberration
The gigantic tattooed bouncer with a sumo hairstyle was smiling
He was always at the gym
As was she
She always acknowledged him
As did he
But this day his face was beaming
Looked completely different
She told him he looked cheery
He thought she was referring to his shirt
No
She said
No
It's you
You're cheery
He grinned
I'm usually grumpy
No I retorted
You're serious
Today you're happy
I'm not the smiley type he said, smiling
She smiled too

She needed to be around people
Gripping the bars
Powering up
She completed her reps

Earnest the Clown

Transferring a slice of pizza to a carry out carton
Perfectly balanced on a knife blade
Nothing could go wrong
Until it did
Unthinkably it flipped over
Overturning assured victory
Snapping into restoration mode
Pepperoni replaced
Edges aligned
No one could tell
She alone knew the inconceivable truth
Sabotaging her skill
Wrecking her record
Sheena was her original clown
Over time
Trying to make life work in her favor
She became Earnest
Seriously loading the dishwasher
The right way
Pizza flop in the box
Saved her with slapstick

Musing

When she first discovered she spoke through music
It thawed her shyness
Broke through the ice
Shattering the surface
Revealing subterranean flow
When she first discovered she spoke through music
Wordlessly connect
Play her harmonica like a drumbeat
Behind a funk guitar
Collaborate with a keyboard
Improvising conversational riffs
Weaving in and out of Summertime
The living was easy
Listening was all that mattered
Not the audience
Not the applause
Not the money
Not the stage
Being seen by being heard

Noise Bomb

Drowning in the band
Cacophonous reverberations
Smothered slices of silence
Killing quiet moments
Listening for interstices
Lost in sound
Melody is mud
Nuance is never
Tone is deaf

Like running a marathon wearing a lead vest
She longed for lightness
For musical connections
Not loud lumbering
Overblown sounds
Slamming into each other
Breaking
What should have been
Sound barrier

Being and Boredom

Mind chattering
To do tasks whiz by
Holding fast to sitting slow
Legs twitching
Mental seatbelt tight
Each inhale deliberate
Stressful
Clenched abdomen resolute
Then a litany of lacks
No meditation practice
No metal sculpture
No writing workshops
No dance classes
No gaggle of girlfriends
Exhausting and not exhaustive
Lists of undone doings
The blob of being fails to intrigue
Becoming one with one's protoplasm
Squeamishly repulsive
Sadly
The pet rock craze is over
Compared to this it would be thrilling

Trash Day

She rummages around in her mind
Flinging
Beyond the confines of her consciousness
Great handfuls of detritus
Making no decisions about what to discard
Getting her whole body into the grabbing and tossing
Myriad piles of costumes
Towering boxes of footwear
Crumpled mounds of sticky notes
Wire coat hangers wielded like weaponry
Twisted into meat hooks
Hanging lengths of fabric like carcasses
Tidying the new roominess
Spewing superlative negatives
Going about the business of transformation
A consummate hoarder
Collecting shards of nascent projects
Scuttled schemes of revenge
Ancient battles
Abandoned victories
She kicks it all away
Wondering as she works
How to live
So emptied

Game Over

I detest rollercoasters
To be hoisted upwards then precipitously dropped
Crashing down breaking the earth's crust
Gathering the splinters
Shoving them into a bag of myself
Reconstituting as I always do

There's a videogame
The object is to break as many bones as possible
The player pitches off a cliff
Attempting to shatter on sheer rock
A pile of breakage marks victory
I adore this game
The violence
The survival
A kind of immortality
Scored destruction
Glorified chaos

Rules

Delighted by their meticulous detail
Each leaf luminous
A dead cicada
Shimmering jade
Consumed by a blanket of yellow jackets
Miraculous moment for the taking
Curiosity is her compass

Arms loaded with groceries
Clearly in need of help
Unused to being noticed
She wheeled a cart to him
Surprised
He accepted her offer

She had certain rules
Cannot rescue a mouse from a cat's pounce
Relocating a slug from a footpath, permitted
Righting an overturned beetle, allowed

Witnessing a mantis devouring a monarch
She froze
Camouflaged by innocence
Patient as a rock

Morphing

In the midst of quietly sitting
Nested in soft green fabric
Sinking into shaggy lawn-like carpet
Ankles grabbed from beneath
Jolts of anxiety rippling
Until she stopped fighting
Let herself expand
Pulled like putty
Spreading out
Curious
She shed her tight skin
Early protection
Worn to obsolescence
In its stead
Left wrinkled and lax
She cried for the loss of her taut casing
But noted the ease of a new roominess
It had been hard to breathe
In the snug smoothness of her old packaging
Though admired
She'd not aspired
Yet nonetheless enjoyed
Despite her fears of visibility
The eyes of others
Now enrobed in crushed velvet
She began to fashion
An elusive wraith
Wrathless

Surreality

She kayaked through the sky
Blue prismatic mirror
Holographic
Surreal illusion
Perfect
Lake of glass
Wishing it would never end
She clung to the magic
Knowing it was fragile
Moved no muscle for fear of shattering the moment
A ruffle of wind
Inevitable
Fragmented the mirage
Drowning it
Nature, take a bow

IV.

Bombay

Backstreets
Magnificent mounds of wreckage
Twisted metal and bare wires sparking
Draping doorways festooned with the faces of gods
Peeling sage and rose and lemon and indigo
Petals showering crystal clouds of pink
Faces cracked with smiles and sorrows
Bodies lithe and limp and dexterous
Dragging legs
Hunchbacked aching eyes
Voluptuous sari-wrapped jeweled forms sliding through crowds
Infinite relentless currents choking passageways
Jostling hustling slumping bustling
Jarring sparring
Catarrh spitting
Beads glistening
Dogs dying
Feet swelling
Chatter aloft on laughter
Nothing lasts

Being

Eyes closed
She sat dutifully
Willing herself to be
Being was elusive
How was it different from doing?
She knew that doing was doing it all wrong
That doing wasn't what it was
But what was it?
She tried breathing on purpose
But that wasn't it
She took off her glasses
The pages were blurry
No closer to being
Was sleep doing or being?
The couch wasn't doing anything
Being
She was certain
Was a stand-alone
Not on the way to something else
Dangerously still
What if she got stuck in the nothingness
Kierkegaardian
Doing and somethingness
Set her sprinting

Detritus

Mucking around in the same old trough
Filled with regurgitated entrails
Troves of vitriol
Caked with scabbed over blood
Lost its fascination
No longer a Garden of Earthly Delights
But an increasingly boring Anatomy Lesson of Dr. Tulp
The present moment sang
Buoyed by crickets chirping
Bullfrog serenades
Skipping rocks across streams
She collected mica
Balanced its fragile mirrors everywhere
Shimmering light on her adobe walls
Inspiring a Oaxacan mole dinner

Reunion

Enormous billowing blooms
Crimson and copper
Undulating lava
Bubbling white-hot steam
Somehow soothing
In rhythm
She danced on the rising shaft of air
Faster than the fire
Unscathed
Unscalded
Seeing clearly through vermillion glasses
Like the yellow tint she'd worn for years to brighten her world
These warmed her
Her two-year-old self toddled toward her
She held her close
Yes
I am your mother

Radical Inclusion

Awkward and confused
The excitement of the playground
Muffled her
Other and alien
Peculiar behavior fascinated her
From recess recluse
She became a psychologist of the unusual
Finding music in the tone deaf
Listening to the noetic
Translating emotional hieroglyphics
Creating communion
With customized bridges and ramps
All can play
Even those whose smiles look like frowns
Whose skin recoils from touch
Whose voices boom big as all outdoors
Whose bodies dance the tarantella
Like one gigantic Alice's Restaurant
You can be anything you want
Even if you don't know what you want
Or what you are
Be one of us

Secret Santa

Partial to completing tasks late at night
Coming upon them the next day
Made her giddy
Someone surprised her by finishing
Her unfinished business
A sneaky friend
Ambitious tooth fairy
Anonymous admirer
What a gift
Transparent as it was
This secret strategy never failed
Invariably she felt enormous relief
Someone had taken care of it
No need to fret
She could take it easy
No one to blame
Modesty aside
No matter how it got done
She had only herself to thank
No time to bask
Off in a flash
She whipped up a Bolognese
Before flopping into bed
Wonder who cooked that up?

Quitting Time

Glimpses of a life led by love
Teased her
She scoffed
Yet when she felt her heart grow warm
Enfolding the world in its embrace
Effervescence bubbled under her step
Floating her aloft
It was decidedly less work to simply love everything and everybody
The relentless task of sorting and discriminating
Winnowing out the deserving from the despicable
She sharpened her claws on the cuttlebone of her critiques
No end to targets available for judgment
No end to the job of dispensing grades
Quitting
Taking it easy
Sloppily loving it all regardless of worth
She waved a tiny white flag

Free-Wheeling

In a tiny little pocket of the world
Dwarfed by empty office buildings
Scarred by militant graffiti
Decayed by not-so-buried hatred
Caked with lies
Living in a community of nobodies
Happily insignificant
Families gather for an ordinary patriotic celebration
Decorated in genuine crepe paper
Scooters join the parade
Earnestly operated by even the youngest citizens
Red, white and blue pompoms adorn bicycles
Lined with crowds of festively outfitted folk
Littered with handfuls of candy flung by merry drivers
Local
Very local
Celebrities
One enormous smile
This precious donut of a moment
Circling cherished residents
Suspending worry and fear and threat
Ignoring politics
Engaging in the spectacular egg toss
Cheered on by neighbors
All buoyed by a bubble of gratitude
Suspended in the hammock of Norman Rockwell patriotism

Saved

Historically sensitive to the slightest chill
She harbored a secret fondness for global warming
Thawing her toes
Frozen in early summer
Then the earth went up in flames
Wildfires
Spread toxic smoke across the continent
Imprisoning humans
Breathing hot humidity drenched air
Constantly soaked with sweat
Melting into the furniture
Unable to concentrate
She found herself imagining the unthinkable
Central air conditioning
The bane of her existence
Now a desperate escape
This was not cozy
Surrendering to artificial cool
She revived
Enlivened
Succumbing to climate control
Then her skin shuddered
Turned cold
Relief morphed to jitters
Feeling the breeze
She started to sneeze
Snaked her hand towards the source
Disempowered the refrigeration
Sank into the sticky morass
Of her personal greenhouse
Flowers bloomed

Transmutation

Impossibly bejeweled
Green and gold glistening
In the exact center of her window
A gigantic perfect cicada displayed neon
Stationary
Permitting examination
Appearing dead
Save for its pulsing luminance.

Later
Honored to find an exoskeleton
Starkly translucent
Hoping to see its freshly pallid occupant
Peering behind the elm
Birthplace of the metamorphosis
She was too late

Practically domesticated
A dragonfly landed on the antenna of her car
Transforming it into a magic wand
Wish granted
Diaphanous flight

Death-Defying

Ancient hands
Hers
Seeing each crease each fold each vein
Sharp relief
Imagining the certainty
Imagining the hovering
Of death
Imagining
For a split second
Being alone as dying eclipses life
How to be unafraid
As darkness draws closer
Shadowing her hands
Leaving her breathless
Trying to escape
Diving into the interior
Finding fire
Flickering
Urgently looking for signs
Of god
Hiding
(Hopefully)
In convolutions
In synapses
In the retina
In the synovial fluid
It would be extraordinarily comforting
Glimpsing god
Even the briefest of flashes
Conjured spiritual transfusion

Playland

She laughs all day
They show her
Flowers
Worms
Buttons
Pinecones
Treasures in need of safekeeping
They tell her secret plans
Squirreling away money
To bring to school
Bring your car they insist
So they can drive it to the grocery store
Where they will buy
Muffins
And this is not a playdate
It is real
She is loved
As a large child person
Not an actual grownup
When she tries to call them to order
They see her as one of their own
A kind adult comes to her rescue
And the kids quiet down
Until she plays her harmonica
Inspires them to dance
Orchestrates their songs
Cheers their agility
Makes mad faces with them
Treasures silliness
Committed to her mission
Always take them seriously

Childlike

Bubble wrap cushions her body
Caught in the chasm
Between touching
And being touched by
The world
Not the whole world
The grown up world
Face to face with a child
The chasm heals
She comes to life
Children melt her mask
She takes their hands
Follows them to their forts
Peels bark money from birch trees
Buries ice in buckets of mud stew
Liking being childlike
In a world where all that truly matters
Is popping the bubbles
Of the wrap

Pinnacle

Her hands and feet were studded snow tires
Gripping the sheer glass face of the summit
Sunbursts bounced from facet to facet
Diamonds danced
Dazzling her
Stopped in her tracks by shafts of light
Magnifying microscopic crystals
Of silicon sand
She pushed against the wind
Desperate to stand alone at the top
A solitary journey
Feared forever
Now
Her mind screams futility
The zeal of her zeitgeist
Surged through her spine
Pulling her upright
Alive against the ice blue sky

Identity

Clandestine spelunking into subterranean crevasses
Formless phosphorescence
Emanated from her
Longing for light that was already hers
She coveted what she already had
Futilely she sought form
To be something
To be somebody
Haunted by a phantom limb
Ancient amputation
Aching for recognition
Anachronistic confetti of identity
Obscured her vision
Like a shaken snow globe

Self-Contained

Attracted to anything that moved
She needed to harness herself to a passion
A grounding passion
Playing
The answer found her
Channeling
Music was her translator
Her true voice
All invitations accepted
Multilingual
World without words
Passion in place
She looked around her room
Concluded she could live there
Forever
Never leaving
Never bored
Journals, photo albums, books
Projects, writing collections
Global travel receipts
Harmonicas
Everywhere she looked
There she was

Flight

Obediently leaden
Rooted to the meditation cushion
Desperate to escape
Everything in the room abruptly tiny
The ceiling far too low
Books thin as pamphlets
Dollhouse size chairs
Strangely free of the cramped body
Slowly she billowed up and out of her small frame
Filling the room
Beyond the ceiling
Soaring upward
She could go on forever
Unfettered
Big and buoyant
Ballooning above the trees
Diving down
She plucked a worm from the grass
Curious to feed a nest-full of hungry-mouthed goldfinch
Loathe to upset the natural order
She delivered it to their mother
Rewarded with a quizzical glance
Watching the entire worm consumption
She kept her distance
Transfixed
Reluctantly wriggling back into her skin
Silk like a parachute

Choice

Sinking into the sumptuous dark mood
Weirdness beckoned
Sucked her into its depths
Lurid demonic image
Tempted her
Resisting
She opened her eyes wide
Light cut through the fog

Choice
She could choose
Happiness
Not weirdness
Light brightened
Opening more space
She could choose

Her guardian rage needed feeding
She gave it a bowl of extra crispy French fries
Walking away
Out of swirling blackness
Into sunshine

The Blue Light

The blue oval glowed
Expanding infinitely
Softly luminous
Shining through her
Dissolved into opalescence
Peace nestled near
Safely succumbing
Edgeless
No anger
No sadness
No fear
Daring to name it
Soul
Grateful for its return
She'd missed its presence
Fearing it had been lost
Forays into the spiritual
Halted by the known
Axed by the rational
Attention on the liminal
Breaking through the veil
She braved the oceanic

About the Author

Carol Moog is a psychologist in private practice, an accomplished blues harmonica player, and the author of *Are They Selling Her Lips* (William Morrow) and *The Autism Playbook for Teens* (New Harbinger). She can also be found improvising with Tongue and Groove Spontaneous Theater, voicing vintage radio plays, and communing with insects on nature walks.

She lives in Pennsylvania with her loving husband and adventure-partner, Roger, with whom she has traveled the world. In lieu of teleportation, she treasures cross-country time with her vibrant daughter, Julie, son-in-law, David, and grandson, Henry.

She has never understood why people tell children to sit still.

Made in the USA
Middletown, DE
23 March 2025